ESSENTIAL TIPS

BONSAI

ESSENTIAL TIPS
101

BONSAI

Harry Tomlinson

DORLING KINDERSLEY
London • New York • Sydney • Moscow
www.dk.com

A DORLING KINDERSLEY BOOK

www.dk.com

Editor Carol Watson
Art Editor Alison Shackleton
Series Editor Charlotte Davies
Series Art Editor Clive Hayball
Production Controller Lauren Britton

First published in Great Britain in 1996 by
Dorling Kindersley Limited,
80 Strand, London WC2R 0RL.

6 8 10 9 7

A CIP catalogue record for this book is available from the British Library

ISBN 0–7513–0361–5

Text film output by The Right Type, Great Britain
Reproduced by Colourscan, Singapore
Printed and bound by Graphicom, Italy

ESSENTIAL TIPS

PAGES 54-57

PROPAGATING BONSAI

PAGES 58-67

SOME SUITABLE SPECIES

PAGES 68-69

DISPLAY & ARRANGEMENT

STARTING OFF A BONSAI

1 WHAT IS BONSAI?

Bonsai is a Japanese expression (*Bon* - shallow tray, *sai* - plant) now used worldwide. It is the name given to an art form, originally Chinese, which is based on a study of trees growing in the wild. Bonsai aims at recreating nature in an idealized miniature landscape.

Heavy bark takes many years to grow

Peeling bark provides interest

Regular clipping creates rounded masses of leaves

◁ SAGERETIA
The attractive foliage and gnarled bark of this tree make it a popular choice for indoor bonsai.

2 WHAT TO LOOK FOR

Most types of tree or shrub are suitable for bonsai. Consider the following characteristics when making your choice:

- An interesting trunk with a good arrangement of branches.
- Attractive bark colour.
- Compact, fine-textured foliage with small leaves, flowers, and fruit (if you want to include them in the design).

Pointed, ribbed, and serrated leaves

Small, glossy evergreen leaves

△ HORNBEAM
A well-balanced trunk with a good taper supports a mass of foliage.

◁ COTONEASTER 'Skogholm', a useful dwarf cotoneaster variety with small evergreen leaves, is shown here in semi-cascade style.

Bright scarlet berries set off the pale blue pot

3 BUYING READY-MADE

The simplest way to acquire a bonsai is to buy one ready-made. For a good variety, try visiting a specialist nursery. Otherwise look carefully around garden centres and general nurseries. The main advantages of buying are that you will have no effort in training and styling, and no lengthy wait to see the final product. The drawbacks are that most ready-made bonsai are expensive imports from Japan, the quality varies, and some trees sold are not true bonsai at all.

4 GARDEN-CENTRE PLANTS

The advantages of this method are: you will have a wide range of species to choose from at prices that are reasonable, you can prune the material to shape quickly, and you can decide the form your bonsai will take. The disadvantage is that the stock is usually grown for garden use, and so may be unsuitable for adapting to bonsai.

Strong, upward-growing branches

The trunk line is now visible

Healthy, dense foliage needs pruning

Roots also have to be pruned

Branches wired in position

BEFORE △
This Chinese Juniper is a six-year-old plant that was bought from a garden centre in order to prune and train.

AFTER △
The front view of the same plant as a bonsai after pruning, and with the trunk and branches wired into position.

5 RESCUING CASTAWAYS

Another cheap way to acquire plants is to collect shrubs that other gardeners no longer want, or have room for. These could be mature trees or bushes that have outgrown their welcome. This discarded stump grew freely for two years. It was then repotted, and eventually the new growth was pruned and wired. Many dwarf plants will adapt to bonsai cultivation, eg. cotoneaster, quince, and pyracantha.

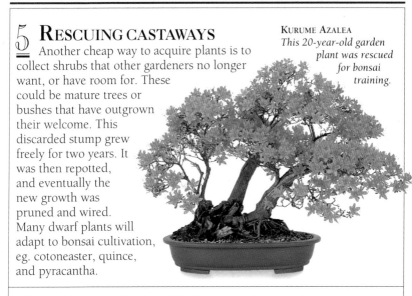

KURUME AZALEA
This 20-year-old garden plant was rescued for bonsai training.

6 COLLECTING FROM THE WILD

In the wild, trees frequently become naturally dwarfed due to climatic or other adverse conditions. You can sometimes lift these and grow them in containers. Of course, it is only appropriate to do this where the plant life would otherwise be lost, and with permission of the landowner. The drawback is it takes a lot of time and effort to find and transport such trees, and even then they may not re-establish.

EUROPEAN BEECH
This tree, trained as bonsai for 14 years in informal upright style, originally formed part of a beech hedge.

7 GROWING FROM SEED

This is inexpensive, but time-consuming as some seed takes two years to germinate, and even then may not germinate well. The main disadvantages of this method are:

- It takes a long time for the tree to develop suitable characteristics for styling as a bonsai.
- The tree may not be "true to" (an exact replica of) the parent plant.

△ **2-YEAR-OLD TREE**
To begin with, grow the seedling in a plastic container.

△ **3-YEAR-OLD TREE**
Keep it here until big enough to plant in open ground.

Branches are stronger

Tree transferred to container

Trunk has now grown thicker

△ **6-YEAR-OLD TREE**
After a few years in open ground the tree is strong and mature enough for pruning and training to begin. Plant it in a container that complements the design.

Branches are bushier after pruning

Trunk is much more mature

10-YEAR-OLD TREE ▷
This Japanese Larch has matured, and with pruning and training has developed an interesting shape. The tree continues to be grown in a container.

8 GROWING FROM CUTTINGS

There are many advantages to this method of cultivation. It is a cheap and easy way to start off a tree, it is true to the parent plant, it can root within six weeks, and in six months grow to the same extent as a three-year old plant grown from seed. The only drawback is that there are some species, such as pines, that are difficult to grow this way.

DWARF HONEYSUCKLE
The 6-year-old trees in this group planting were grown from cuttings.

9 GRAFTING & AIR LAYERING

These are two other ways of propagating that produce results much more quickly than growing from seed, and also carry forward the correct characteristics of the parent plant. The disadvantage of these methods is that they require a high level of dexterity and skill, and are not therefore ideal for those just beginning bonsai.

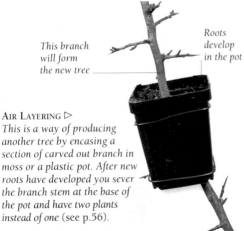

This branch will form the new tree

Roots develop in the pot

AIR LAYERING ▷
This is a way of producing another tree by encasing a section of carved out branch in moss or a plastic pot. After new roots have developed you sever the branch stem at the base of the pot and have two plants instead of one (see p.56).

△ **GRAFTING**
A young branch is fixed onto older rootstock in order to grow a new plant with the maturity of the old (see p.57).

DESIGN PRINCIPLES

10 CREATING A BALANCE

A good design has an overall balance, achieved by shaping and training the structure of the tree, and the relationship of the tree to container. There are three main factors to consider: the root spread, the form of the trunk, and the arrangement of the branches.

The taper balances the thickness of the trunk base

The tree's shape changes from conical to flat-topped as it ages

Remove cones to preserve the design element

Arrangement of branches balances trunk

Smooth, grey bark becomes rugged with age

JAPANESE
WHITE PINE

11 ROOT SPREAD

An interesting formation of exposed roots adds to the impression of the tree's character and maturity. This is one of the most interesting features of bonsai, giving an air of age and stability.

For the most pleasing visual effect the roots should extend from the trunk in many different directions, either flowing away from it or providing the trunk with a firm buttress or anchorage.

VISIBLE ROOT SPREAD

THICK, MATURE TRUNK

12 TRUNK

The most important feature of the trunk is a good taper (narrow towards the tip). Thickness at the base adds maturity, but a parallel trunk line destroys the balance of the design. Whatever the angle the trunk grows in, it is vital to have a good view of the trunk line. Look for bark with texture and colour as these add character, and an aged, weathered appearance is attractive. Avoid scarred or damaged bark.

13 ARRANGEMENT OF BRANCHES

Branches form the basic structure of the tree's silhouette. You can alter this by pruning and wiring, but still look out for certain basic features when choosing a tree or shrub. Aim for an arrangement that flows up and around the tree like a spiral staircase, forming a balanced pattern around the trunk. The first and heaviest branch level should be a third of the way up the trunk, and ideally each branch should taper away from the trunk and narrow towards its end.

14 WHICH VIEWPOINT?

Always design a bonsai with one preferred viewing angle, called a "front view". This should display the most graceful angle and taper of the trunk, an attractive aspect of the root structure, and the most pleasing arrangement of branches. Your eye-level should correspond to a point half-way up the trunk.

Tree has an elegant, tapering trunk

Apex should lean towards the viewer

△ LEFT SIDE

The horizontal spread is helped by wiring

△ RIGHT SIDE

FRONT VIEW ▷

Tree placed off-centre to balance the design

JAPANESE WHITE PINE
This well-balanced, asymmetrical shape has a clean outline and good view of the trunk.

△ BACK VIEW

15 SIZE & SCALE

Most bonsai are between 15 cm (6 in) and 60 cm (2 ft) in height. The small-leaved trees are more adaptable in terms of scale, and dwarf tree forms are excellent for styling on rock. Group plantings offer more scope for a sense of scale because the trees relate to each other, and to other elements of the design, such as rocks and ground cover.

CLASPED-TO-ROCK STYLE

16 TREE & CONTAINER

Consider the size and proportion of the pot in relation to the tree, the overall character of the design, and the position of the tree within the container. This must be in scale with the tree, enhancing the balance of the tree's height and spread. Match the texture and type of container to the style of the tree. Elegant trees need dainty containers; rugged trees usually demand plain, heavy pots.

SWISS WILLOW

17 WHAT TO AVOID

Certain types of branch growth do not make good design elements. Prune these out. Avoid branches that cross, spread out from the same point on the trunk, or grow directly opposite one another at the same level on the trunk. You can adjust the direction of these branches with wiring techniques (see p.39). Large leaves and coarse foliage and twigs are also difficult to work with.

BONSAI STYLES

18 COPYING NATURE

With bonsai, you can recreate the sense of perspective, strength, and durability of full-size trees on a scale that is manageable. The most important principle of bonsai styling is to ensure all specimens are based on the ways trees grow in nature. There are five basic styles: formal upright, informal upright, semicascade, cascade, and slanting styles. These represent the angle of the trunk. The fifteen styles here represent the full range of bonsai design in single-trunk, multiple trunk, and group plantings.

△ ROOT-OVER-ROCK STYLE
This technique recreates a form of natural growth seen with the exposed roots of trees in rocky or mountainous areas.

◁ ROOTS IN NATURE
The exposed roots of a Silver Birch grip the rock as they search for nourishment and water from the soil.

19 FORMAL UPRIGHT STYLE

The tree grows straight and upright. In nature this happens when the tree is in an ideal, open situation, with plenty of water, nourishment, and no adverse weather conditions. The trunk of the bonsai tree should have an even taper from base to tip, and the shape of the branches should form a well-balanced silhouette. Suitable species: pines (*Pinus*), junipers (*Juniperus*), and spruces (*Picea*).

The spread of the branches is not symmetrical

JAPANESE LARCH

20 INFORMAL UPRIGHT STYLE

This style is the most commonly seen, both in nature and bonsai. Due to environmental factors – wind, shade, and competition for light or moisture from other plants and buildings – the trunk of a tree curves, bends, and changes direction. The growth of the trunk is basically upright and vertical (or within approximately 15° of vertical), with a well-balanced silhouette. The majority of species is suitable.

The slant of the trunk is viewed from the front

SILVER BIRCH

21 SEMICASCADE STYLE

In nature you see waterside trees like this. To qualify for this style, the trunk should appear to be almost horizontal, even if the plant grows a little below the level of the pot rim. You can train many species of tree or shrub in this way.

JAPANESE FLOWERING CHERRY

22 CASCADE STYLE

This style represents a tree growing on a mountainside. The bonsai trunk line falls below the horizontal, with the trunk ending below the level of the pot. This style is suitable for all trees except those with a strong upright growth.

PYRACANTHA

23 BROOM STYLE

This restrained classic bonsai style is difficult to achieve. Named after an upturned Japanese broom, the straight section of the trunk supports a domed head of twiggy branches. Recommended species: fine-branched deciduous trees, such as elm (*Ulmus*).

JAPANESE ELM

24 LITERATI STYLE

This style (also called *bunjin*), is seen at the seashore or in areas where trees grow up reaching for the light. The trunk line flows or twists through several curves and the trees have an air of refined elegance.

The style takes its inspiration from the paintings of Chinese scholars called *wenjen*, translated by the Japanese as *bunjin*. The word "literati" (derived from the Latin for "literate people") is used as an equivalent term. Recommended species: conifers and deciduous trees like hawthorn (*Crataegus*).

JAPANESE
BLACK PINE

25 SLANTING STYLE

In nature trees grow in this way when reaching out for light or away from buffeting winds. The trunk can be curved or straight, but leans at a definite angle from base to tip (usually to a maximum of 45° from the vertical). The roots act as anchorage, growing out away from the leaning tree and compressed beneath it on the opposite side. Most species suit this style.

MOUNTAIN
PINE

21

26 ROOT-OVER-ROCK STYLE

This happens in nature when trees establish themselves in crevices and rocky ledges and need to send out roots to find moisture and nourishment in deeper soil.

In bonsai design the main feature of interest is a "close-up" of the roots clinging to the rock. Choose trees with naturally strong roots that also grow easily on rock. Recommended species: Chinese Elm (*Ulmus parvifolia*), junipers, and pines.

TRIDENT MAPLE

27 CLASPED-TO-ROCK STYLE

DWARF JAPANESE WHITE PINE

This style represents trees in nature that grow on mountains and cliffs and can be designed for "near" or "distant" views. The roots are confined only to the rock and do not extend into the soil of the pot, so it is vital to water regularly.

Use a flat piece of slate for planting in the same way as a pot, or a rugged rock displayed in a shallow tray (*suiban*) of sand or water. Recommended species are trees that are known to grow in mountainous areas, such as juniper, pine, birch, and spruce.

28 TWIN-TRUNK STYLE

A familiar sight in nature, this arises when a tree develops two trunks from the base of the same root system. Usually, one trunk predominates, and this is essential in your bonsai design. The trunks may divide at, or just above soil level; sometimes you can train a low branch and style it as a second trunk. The same principle applies to any style with more than one trunk. Recommended species: birch (*Betula*), beech (*Fagus*), and Japanese Cedar (*Cryptomeria*).

JAPANESE RED MAPLE

29 CLUMP STYLE

This is where several trunks grow from the same root in a clump formation, spreading out from the base as each one reaches out for its own light. Many clumps exist in old English woodlands where trees were coppiced (sawn off at the ground to grow straight poles to be used for fencing).

JAPANESE KURUME AZALEA

30 STRAIGHT-LINE STYLE

JAPANESE DECIDUOUS HOLLY

Also known as raft style, this is based on a tree in nature that has fallen or blown over, but continues to grow — the original branches reaching up vertically to become trunks.

In bonsai this provides scope for you to make interesting designs out of poor trees with one-sided branches, material that you could not use for a single specimen bonsai. The long, slender branches of this Japanese deciduous holly are a perfect example. The design of the tree and colour of the berries is complemented by the beige, flat, shallow container.

31 SINUOUS STYLE

DWARF JAPANESE FLOWERING QUINCE

This style occurs in nature when suckers arise from surface roots of a tree, or where a very low branch rubs on the ground, roots into the soil and then produces other smaller trunks. Recommended species: trees with flexible trunks, such as pine (*Pinus*), and yew (*Taxus*), or trees with a tendency to throw up suckers from exposed roots such as elm (*Ulmus*) and quince (*Chaenomeles*).

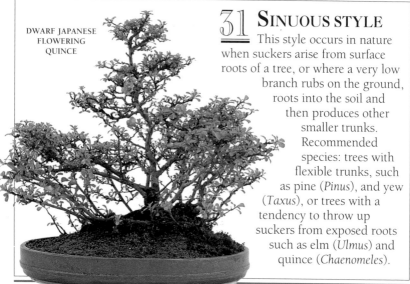

32 SAIKEI PLANTING

Also known as "tray landscape", this is a way of presenting a natural landscape (such as your favourite view) in miniature form. You can use each of the materials for a short-term composition, then promote the trees to individual bonsai as they become mature.

DWARF HINOKI CYPRESS

33 GROUP PLANTING

This method of planting recreates the effect of a spinney, wood, or forest — with several trees growing together. The style must look natural and uncontrived, and is easier to achieve if you use odd numbers of trees. Most species are suitable for group planting.

UKON MAPLE

YEAR-ROUND COLOUR

34 SPRING DISPLAY

Spring is an exciting time of the year in bonsai cultivation. The bright green, new needles of the Japanese Larch (*Larix kaempferi*), and the brilliant foliage of the Japanese maples (*Acer palmatum*) are just some of the colours on show.

OTHER SUGGESTED SPECIES:
Azalea (Rhododendron), wisteria, crab apple (Malus), hawthorn (Crataegus), Autumn Cherry (Prunus subhirtella 'Autumnalis'), and other cherries.

DESHÔJÔ MAPLE

35 SUMMER DISPLAY

At this time bonsai grow vigorously. Fresh new leaves provide a variety of greens, and flowering trees have spectacular coloured blooms, such as those of the many azaleas (*Rhododendron*).

OTHER SUGGESTED SPECIES:
Summer-flowering Pomegranate (Punica granatum), pyracantha, and cotoneasters.

SATSUKI AZALEA

36 Autumn Display

This season is just as colourful as spring, because the leaves of the deciduous trees change hue. The maples (*Acer*) display a wonderful range of yellow, orange, red, and purple leaves. The needles of the larch (*Larix*) change from bright green to vivid gold; ginkgo leaves turn buttercup yellow, and you will see some of the most brilliant shades of red on the leaves of all types of stewartia and euonymus.

OTHER SUGGESTED SPECIES:
Rowan (Sorbus aucuparia), crab apple, Japanese Deciduous Holly (Ilex serrata), beech (Fagus), birch (Betula), and some cotoneasters.

ENGLISH ELM

37 Winter Display

JAPANESE BLACK PINE

This is the time to view evergreens such as the bright green needles of this Japanese Black Pine (*Pinus thunbergii*). Later in the season the pale, fragrant blossoms of the Flowering Apricot (*Prunus mume*) come into bloom one of the most colourful trees of winter.

OTHER SUGGESTED SPECIES:
Chinese Quince (Chaenomeles sinensis), Winter Jasmine (Jasminum nudiflorum), Stewartia, and Crape Myrtle (Lagerstroemia indica).

USEFUL TOOLS

38 PRUNING & CUTTING TOOLS

There are many tools available on the market — some highly specialized for the expert. Good tools are expensive, but cheaper ones are of inferior quality and a false economy. When you buy tools consider the type and size of bonsai you wish to work with.

- Large trees require large, strong tools.
- Small trees need fine, delicate tools.

△ TURNTABLE

△ CONCAVE
BRANCH CUTTER

△ SPHERICAL
KNOB CUTTER

TRIMMING
SHEARS ▷

LONG-HANDLED
SHEARS ▷

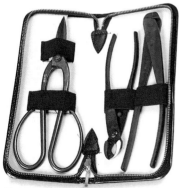

WOUND
SEALANT ▷

◁ CUT PASTE

BASIC TOOL SET △
This contains a wire cutter, and two essential pruning tools: trimming shears, and a concave branch cutter.

39 WIRING TOOLS

You use wire not only to train the branches and trunks of trees (see pp.38–39), but also to anchor them firmly in place in their containers (see p.50), or on rock plantings (see p.43). The pliers have a dual function — they twist anchorage wires into shape and position, and also treat wood on the trunk to make jins (see p.41).

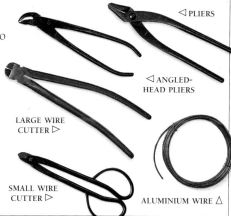

◁ PLIERS

◁ ANGLED-HEAD PLIERS

LARGE WIRE CUTTER ▷

SMALL WIRE CUTTER ▷

ALUMINIUM WIRE △

40 POTTING TOOLS & EQUIPMENT

These tools are all used for potting trees at the beginning of their life as bonsai, and then after that for the regular repotting that forms an essential part of routine maintenance (see p.50). The mesh is used to cover the drainage holes in the pot (see p.31) to prevent the soil from seeping out of the container when watering the plant.

△ BRUSH   △ POTTING TROWEL   △ MESH   △ ROOT HOOK   △ SOIL SCOOP

41 POWER TOOLS

You may sometimes need to use power tools when pruning very heavy tree trunks. The two most versatile are the die grinder, which is a carving tool that is easy to control, and the rotary tool with flexible drive. Use this to refine carving carried out with the die grinder, or instead of it when working on smaller trees.

HOW TO CREATE A BONSAI

42 CHOOSING THE RIGHT CONTAINER

Always choose the container after styling the tree. Find one that complements it in size, shape, colour, and finish, and consider the following practical points:

- The pot should drain easily, but also allow enough moisture to be retained to keep the tree healthy.
- It must hold enough soil for the tree roots to develop.
- It should be frost-proof.

△ MAME POTS
These are extremely small decorated pots that vary in size from only 12 mm (½ in) up to 40 mm (1½ in).

◁ SELECTION OF POTS
Below are some of the many shapes, sizes and colours of pot available.

43 CONTAINER STYLES

All bonsai specialist nurseries offer an attractive range of container styles with a wide variety of size, shape, and detail. Most are good quality, mass-produced or handmade bonsai pots imported from the Tokoname region of Japan. Bonsai pots usually come in natural earth colours with a glazed or unglazed finish and unglazed interior.

△ UNGLAZED POT

△ OVAL MATT-GLAZED "ONYX" POT

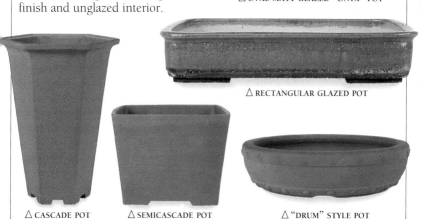

△ RECTANGULAR GLAZED POT

△ CASCADE POT   △ SEMICASCADE POT   △ "DRUM" STYLE POT

44 PREPARING A POT

A good bonsai pot has large holes to allow free drainage of moisture. To prevent the soil being washed away, fix small rectangles of plastic mesh over the drainage holes with wires. Make these by cutting a length of wire and forming each end into a loop with a short tail. Push the tails of wire up through the mesh and flatten them out to hold it in place.

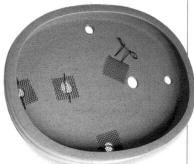

CONTAINER WITH PLASTIC MESH

45 PRUNING TO SHAPE

The simplest, quickest way to create a bonsai is to buy a small garden centre shrub, such as a cotoneaster or a pyracantha, and prune it into shape. Choose one with a sturdy, thick trunk, a good trunk line, plenty of branches, and compact twigs or foliage.

COTONEASTER

1 △ With a root hook, gently loosen the soil in the rootball and comb out the roots. Carefully disentangle and then prune all the longer roots, and remove any that grow downwards. Now turn the shrub around at eye level to ascertain which is the best view for the front of the bonsai.

2 ▷ Prune away the twiggy growth to expose the trunk line. Shorten all the branches, but leave an interesting structure for new foliage to grow close to the trunk. Repot the pruned tree in a suitable container that complements and balances the bonsai design.

46 CLIP & GROW

This is a two-stage process that you can follow to develop a bonsai with a more dramatic design, and also to encourage an aged or rugged appearance. Drastic pruning precedes a period of regrowth. This then produces results in the following season. Always choose a plant with a sturdy trunk and vigorous growth. Turn it round and study it carefully from every side before deciding on the most attractive viewing angle (see p.16). The autumn-flowering cherry shown here was originally bought as a shrub from a garden centre, and approximately one year has elapsed since it was first pruned into this shape.

FLOWERING CHERRY

1 △ Prune back the shrub's fibrous roots and shorten heavy roots to create a compact root system at the trunk base.

2 △ Cut off unwanted branches, leaving each wound with a small stub from which new shoots can develop.

3 △ Apply wound sealant to keep moisture in the trunk, and plant in a training pot. Leave for one year.

47 PRUNING & WIRING

It is easy to create a bonsai just by pruning dwarf conifers or shrubs. With taller-growing trees, however, you may need to grow your own specimen from seed or a cutting. As you work on styling the tree, you may find it necessary to use wire to control the structure and development of the bonsai; so it is with this Japanese White Pine.

1 △ When the tree is ready for pruning, comb the roots with a metal root hook. Shorten them enough for the plant to fit the container.

2 △ Choose the front view of the bonsai. Refine the structure by pruning unnecessary branches from the trunk using concave branch cutters.

3 △ Continue until half the foliage from the tree has been removed. Leave a stub at the base of the trunk in order to create a jin later.

4 △ Once you have pruned the tree into the basic bonsai shape, adjust the trunk line and branches by wiring to create a more attractive silhouette.

FINAL STAGE
The removal of old needles and downward-hanging foliage has refined and clarified the horizontal lines. The styling has created a graceful branch structure.

Wiring twists the tree top into shape

Naturally strong trunk line

Horizontal lines are emphasized by wiring

Rugged bark adds character

A jin gives an aged look to the tree

Tree is slightly off-centre in pot to balance design

35

48 RESHAPING BY WIRING

With this technique you can shape a tree by changing the direction of the trunk and branches. Upward-growing branches can become horizontal or sweep downwards to give an impression of age and maturity.

- Wire evergreens at any time (but the best time for conifers is from late autumn to early spring).
- Wire deciduous trees in late spring (before leaf buds open) or autumn (before dormancy).
- Practise on junipers – the wood is flexible and unlikely to snap.

BEFORE WIRING
The tree branches have a strong, upward growth and dense foliage.

1 △ Choose the front view of the tree. Cut off the heavy branches near the tree's base, and then thin out the upper branches a little.

2 △ Cut a piece of wire a third longer than the combined lengths of the two lowest branches. Wind the wire around the trunk to anchor it.

3 △ Turn the wire once over the lowest branch, around the trunk, and then around the other branch. Wire the length of each branch.

Well-shaped foliage pads will fill out later

OVERALL DESIGN
On this species the wiring remains in place for one year. Inspect regularly and remove wires if they bite into the bark. After that re-wire the tree every 2–3 years.

Branches wired horizontally

The graceful trunk line is now visible

Stubs should be treated as jins

AFTER WIRING
After pruning and wiring all the branches and trunk, and repotting in a suitable container (see pp.33, 38, & 50), the juniper has the skeleton of a handsome bonsai.

49 STARTING TO WIRE THE TRUNK

You will need to be able to wire neatly and accurately, so do invest time in mastering the technique. Make sure you have wire-cutters, pliers, and wire in the gauges you need. Cut your wire a third as long again as the branch or trunk you intend to work on, so you can wind it round at a 45° angle — the best for effective wiring.

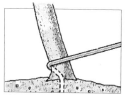

1 △ Push one end of the wire into the soil, then bend the wire round the base of the trunk.

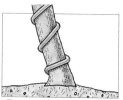

2 △ Wind the first coil of wire around the trunk base. Continue to wind up the trunk.

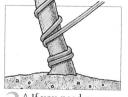

3 △ If you need more than one wire, wind it close to the second, but do not cross wires.

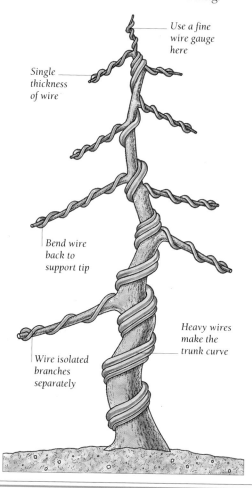

Use a fine wire gauge here

Single thickness of wire

Bend wire back to support tip

Wire isolated branches separately

Heavy wires make the trunk curve

50 BRANCH WIRING

Start wiring from the lowest level upwards. Either wire the length of each branch alternately until you have completed the whole tree (returning to the finer twigs for detailed wiring), or finish one branch at a time with both the main wire and subsidiary wiring before moving on. Use thinner wire as the thickness of branch tapers.

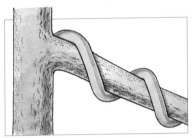

1 △ Start to wire a branch by taking the first turn of the wire over the branch. If the wire goes underneath, the branch may snap when bent.

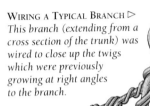

WIRING A TYPICAL BRANCH ▷
This branch (extending from a cross section of the trunk) was wired to close up the twigs which were previously growing at right angles to the branch.

Finer wire gauge here at twig tip

Wire trains the twig inwards

Twig now forms V-shape

This piece of wire acts as an anchor

2 △ Usually you wire two branches at the same time with one piece of wire, wrapping it around the trunk in between to give the wire anchorage.

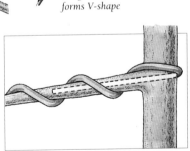

3 △ Where a branch is too isolated to wire in conjunction with another, secure the end of the wire by trapping it under the first few turns.

51 HOW LONG TO LEAVE THE WIRE

This depends on the thickness of the trunk or branch, the type of tree, and the quality and age of the wood. Check wiring regularly to make sure it does not begin to cut into the bark as the tree grows and thickens. A flexible, young branch will hold its position more quickly than older wood. Leave the wiring in place for three to six months with deciduous trees, and six to twelve months for evergreens.

WIRE SCARRING
This branch has been deeply scarred by wire that was left in place too long.

52 CHANGING THE WIRE GAUGE

Wire may be many different gauges (thicknesses). Be careful to match the wire gauge to the size and vigour of the wood. As the thickness of the trunk or branch tapers towards the tip, you need to change the wire to a smaller gauge. The recommended size of wire gauge is between one-sixth and one-third the diameter of the wood wired, but you must also consider the wood's age and pliability.

REMOVING THE WIRE
There is less damage to the tree if you cut the wire away in very small pieces.

53 REMOVING THE WIRE

Do this by unwinding the wire, or preferably by cutting it away in small pieces, reducing the risk of damage to the tree. Wire left too long will bite into the bark. If this happens, unwind it very carefully, following its original direction. If there are any deep cuts, paint them with wound sealant. After removing the wire make sure the tree does not revert to its former position.

54 CREATING A JIN

Trees in nature often have dead wood attached, giving them a dramatic appearance. In bonsai this is reflected in driftwood style, *shari* (torn wood on trunk) or *jins*.

A jin gives the impression of age and makes the tree look as if it has been naturally damaged. Create a jin by stripping the bark off a cut or pruned branch stub.

1 △ Use a concave branch cutter to score the bark around the base of the stub. Crush the bark with jinning pliers to separate it from the wood.

2 △ Grip the loosened bark with the jinning pliers and carefully pull it away from the stub. This will expose the white wood underneath.

3 △ To create a more natural effect, grip the wood with the jinning pliers and tear it downwards to expose the grain and create the desired shape.

4 △ When you are satisfied with the appearance of the jin, use a wire brush (manual or electric) to clean up the surface of the exposed wood.

55 PLANTING ON ROCK

You can bring an extra dimension to the art of bonsai by using rock. The key to success is to combine a beautiful piece of rock with an interesting and attractive tree planting. Use a large, single rock to represent a mountain, craggy cliff, or rocky island; or place several small rocks in a container to create a rocky terrain. A slab of rock or slate instead of a container makes the design look especially natural.

56 CHOOSING A ROCK

There are many types of rock, but some are more suitable than others for bonsai planting. Avoid quartz and marble (bright, glittery textures), sandstone, and other soft, sedimentary rocks (frost might make them split). The best kind of rock for bonsai is a hard rock that will not crumble away. Choose one with an interesting and attractive shape, texture, and colour.

57 MATERIALS FOR ROCK PLANTING

For rock planting you will need the following materials: a selection of trees and rocks, anchorage wires, moss (soaked in water for several hours before use), strong, waterproof adhesive, and peat muck. For root-over-rock style you will also need plastic grafting tape.

VIEWPOINTS
Always choose the aspect of the rock that has the most character to form the front view of your design, as with the piece of Japanese Ibigawa rock on the left.

Variations in colour and texture

ANCHORAGE WIRES
Long ends on either side of a small circle of wire secure the tree when planting.

58 PLANTING CLASPED-TO-ROCK STYLE

THE FINAL PLANTING
This gives an immediate impression of a dramatic landscape.

The most important part of the design is the rock, and the shape and proportion of the plants should complement its features. Carefully study the rock's shape and type. Select one that has an interesting, but natural-looking shape. Then choose appropriate plants. For a rugged rock use mountainside trees such as pine, birch, juniper, or spruce. A smooth, rounded rock suggests a watery scene, and needs waterside trees like willows.

1 △ Glue the prepared anchorage wires to the places on the rock where you intend to plant each of your trees.

2 △ Spread the roots of each tree over a layer of peat muck, pressed onto the rock in position. Cover with more muck.

3 △ To hold the tree in place, cross the anchorage wires over the roots. Fasten by twisting the wire ends together.

59 PLANTING ROOT-OVER-ROCK

This style focuses on the roots of the tree which reach out to the soil for nourishment. Choose trees that naturally form strong surface roots such as Chinese Elm and Trident Maple. The choice of rock is important too, as the tree's roots fuse with it in order to make it a permanent part of the planting. You will need a hard, craggy, frost-resistant rock that is interesting in both shape and texture.

1 △ Gently comb out the tree roots. Then choose a rock which matches the shape formed by the roots. Wrap them in position over the rock.

2 △ While you hold the tree in place, ask a helper to bandage the roots tightly to the rock with plastic tape. Leave the longer roots free at the base.

3 △ Prune the tree hard, to within no more than 1–2 buds from the trunk, and seal the ends of the cut branches to keep the moisture in the tree.

4 △ Plant the rock and roots in a pot of sharp sand, covering the base of the trunk. Leave at least one year until the roots cling securely to the rock.

After a few months the tree will come into leaf

THE FINAL RESULT
After one year's regular watering, the roots should have developed properly. Remove the tree from the pot of sand, choose a front view and plant in a container full of soil. Cover with moss.

The weight of the rock balances the slender tree

60 GROUP PLANTING

With this style it is important to create an illusion of distance and space. Always select trees of the same species, evergreen or deciduous. For small- to medium-sized groups choose trees with small leaves, but use larger-leaved, coarse-growing trees for bigger groups.

The tallest tree leans forwards slightly

All trunks are clearly visible from the front

JAPANESE
DWARF CEDAR

1 △ Select your trees then comb and trim the roots to fit the pot. Decide the front view of the tallest tree and position near the front.

2 ▷ Plant shorter and thinner trees on either side of the first. Vary the spacing between them and tilt them to make them look natural.

3 △ Groom the foliage and water the soil well. Add fresh moss to complete the natural effect. Use a spatula to settle it firmly in place.

61 SAIKEI PLANTING

Saikei (living landscape) is a combination of living plants and materials such as rock, soil, sand, and moss. You can create any type of landscape as long as the plants of your choice are able to flourish together in that environment. Make sure that the different components blend harmoniously.

1 △ Choose the rocks you want to use and position them in the container. Leave a space between them to give the landscape a sense of perspective.

2 △ Plant trees in potting soil behind a large rock. Add ground cover plants of different heights and textures around the base of the trees.

3 △ Trim heathers in such a way that they resemble the trees; they will appear further away. Plant them behind a smaller rock to give a sense of depth.

THE FINISHED PLANTING

Heathers represent trees growing on distant rocks

Soil covered with moss and ground cover

CARING FOR YOUR PLANTS

62 WHICH POSITION?

Three main factors should determine the bonsai's position:
- A favourable viewpoint.
- The right conditions for healthy growth for that particular species (sun or shade, humidity levels).
- The best conditions for working with your plants (watering, pruning, and training).

OUTDOOR DISPLAY

63 WATERING ROUTINE

This is the most important factor in the successful cultivation of bonsai. Unless otherwise specified, water daily as required throughout spring, summer, and autumn. Watch carefully in the winter and always keep your plants moist.

64 WHEN TO WATER

The best time to water plants is in the evening, after the sun has gone down. The moisture then remains in the soil, available to the roots overnight. If you water during the day the soil could dry out after a few hours, and water droplets may cause leaf scorch.

65 HOW TO WATER

Watering is best done from above using either a watering can or a hosepipe. Water indoor plants outside, and drain well before returning to their inside location.

- The watering can needs a long neck to provide a sufficient force of water for an adequate spray.
- The hosepipe needs a fine rose on the end to avoid plant damage.

66 WHICH SOIL MIXTURE?

The essential requirement for all bonsai potting mixtures is that they are able to drain freely. Different trees require different soil, but in general a standard mixture would consist of one part loam, two parts peat, and two parts coarse grit.

67 FEEDING BONSAI

In order for bonsai plants to thrive, you must feed them.
- Liquid fertilizer is quick-acting, but it is difficult to detect how much has been absorbed.
- Solid fertilizer (powder, blocks, granules, and cakes) is better as you can see when to re-fertilize.

68 ROOT PRUNING

This gives the tree an opportunity to grow more strongly because new feeder roots develop in the soil. Repot trees that are vigorous growers, such as larch, annually. The usual time for this is spring, but you can root prune hardy trees in mid- to late winter providing the soil is not frozen. Shorten the roots by about one third. This allows space in the pot to add enough fresh potting soil for healthy growth.

INSPECTING THE ROOT BALL
Cut the anchorage wires and tilt the tree. The encircling roots show it requires pruning.

1 △ Comb out the roots with a metal root hook. Avoid damage to the radial roots which show on the surface.

2 △ Once disentangled, you can see the length of the root mass. Cut away all this length when root pruning.

3 △ Next, cut wedge-shaped pieces out of the rootball to encourage fibrous root-growth close to the trunk of the tree.

69 REPOTTING

The purpose of repotting a bonsai tree is to give a greater area of soil in which the pruned roots can make further growth. As the bonsai pot is a part of the overall design, you usually put the tree back in the same container once the roots are cut back. Before starting, prepare some anchorage wires and squares of plastic mesh.

1 △ Wash the container and cover the drainage holes with plastic mesh. Insert the prepared anchorage wire through one hole and back up another.

2 △ Leave long ends on the wire ready to secure the tree in place. Bend these back before spreading fresh soil mixture across the base of the pot.

3 △ Position the tree on the soil to give the correct front view. Bring the anchorage wires across the rootball. Twist together with pliers to secure.

4 △ Add more soil and gently work into the root mass until the container is full. Water well and lay moist moss over the surface of the soil.

70 SCISSOR TRIMMING

This is carried out through the growing season to refine the shape of the tree and to encourage bushier growth. Always trim the stems, not the foliage as this would make the leaves turn brown at the edges and look untidy. If you prefer, use your fingernails rather than a pair of scissors to prune out the very soft, young shoots.

1 △ Hold the top of the shoot and cut through the stem just above the leaf. You can either throw the cutting away or use it for propagation.

2 △ Cut off all the long shoots that extend out from the silhouette of the tree to leave a compact shape. This makes the tree look more mature.

Trim upper shoots early enough to prevent thickening

Trimming the ends encourages growth further back

BEFORE TRIMMING

AFTER TRIMMING

71 LEAF CUTTING

With some species it is possible to remove all the leaves in summer in order to force a second crop of leaves in autumn. These are smaller, and brighter than the first flush. New leaves develop from buds already formed for next year. Leaf cut soon after these buds have appeared so the new leaves can "harden off" before autumn.

1 △ Start leaf cutting at the top of the tree and work downwards.

2 △ Cut just behind the leaf, leaving the stalk still on the branch.

3 △ Leave leaf stalks to preserve moisture for the dormant buds below.

72 FINGER PRUNING

Pinching back (finger-pruning) and trimming of terminal growth causes secondary growth further back on the twig or branch. This increases the bushiness and fullness of the foliage, and gives the tree a more mature appearance. Always finger-prune the most vigorous upper branches of the tree to stop it becoming top heavy.

1 △ To prune needle-like foliage hold the shoot as shown above.

2 △ Pull the shoot straight towards you in a quick movement.

FINGER PRUNING SCALE-LIKE FOLIAGE
Prune scale-like foliage, (cypress and some junipers) differently. Grip the leading shoot at an angle and twist as you pull the shoot out. This makes a clean break and does not damage the rest of the foliage.

73 PESTS & DISEASES

As with all trees, bonsai sometimes fall prey to pests and diseases. To help prevent problems, spray monthly from spring through summer with a systemic insecticide and fungicide. Do this either when the leaves are in bud, or after they have fully opened (not when the leaves are unfurling as you might damage the soft, new leaves).

BLACKFLY
These aphids are common pests which suck the sap of the tree and spread diseases. If you spot them, spray the tree.

LEAFMINER LEAF DAMAGE
This shows as brown or white markings on the leaf surface. Remove the damaged leaves and spray with insecticide.

GREENFLY
You often find these on thin-leaved, deciduous trees. They lurk under the leaves and secrete a sticky "honeydew".

VINE WEEVIL LEAF DAMAGE
Vine weevils attack leaves and roots. The larvae can live in the soil up to six months. Soak pots in a solution of gamma-HCH.

CUCKOO SPIT
Globules of white froth on leaves and shoots contain insect larvae which damage the plant. Spray with insecticide.

PROPAGATING BONSAI

74 SOWING SEEDS

This needs time and space. Check the required species is one that can be propagated from seed, and that the seeds are fresh. Collect them yourself or buy them from a good seed merchant. Do not buy "bonsai kits" as they are costly and often unreliable. Sow the seeds in early autumn or winter, and protect from birds and rodents.

1 △ Fill a seed tray with a suitable soil mixture. Then sprinkle a layer of sand over the soil to make the seeds visible.

2 △ Make narrow furrows in the surface of the sand, and place the seeds in the furrows, spacing them out evenly.

3 △ Cover over completely with a layer of coarse grit, water well, and leave outside in the open for a year.

75 TRANSPLANTING SEEDLINGS

After one year, gently remove each seedling from the tray and trim back the long, straggly roots. Keep the fine, fibrous roots close to the stem base. Fill a 7.5 cm (3 in) plastic plant pot with a free-draining soil mix, and plant one seedling in it. Repeat with each seedling. Pot them on annually for several years.

PINE SEEDLING

76 TAKING CUTTINGS

This method of propagation is easy and reliable, and new plants created this way always have the same characteristics as their parents. There are two kinds of cuttings — softwood (current season's growth), and hardwood (fully ripened wood).

WATERING & LABELLING ▷
Label with the name and date of the cuttings, and water regularly.

1 △ Gently hold the cutting material upright, and use sharp scissors to snip it cleanly off the parent plant.

2 △ Remove the side shoots and needles from the bottom third of the cutting to prevent it rotting under the soil.

3 △ Make a hole in the soil of a prepared pot. Insert the cutting in the hole and firmly press the soil down around it.

77 POTTING UP CUTTINGS

Keep your cuttings for one year in an unheated glasshouse or cold frame, watering regularly. After this you will see considerable growth, with roots appearing out of the drainage holes. To pot up your cuttings, carefully lift each one from the container, trim the long roots, and replant in a 7.5 cm (3 in) plant pot using free-draining soil mix. Grow on for another year before planting out in the open.

78 HOW TO AIR LAYER

It is possible to produce a bonsai comparatively quickly using this method, as you can choose a suitable, well-shaped branch for your tree before the process begins.

You can air layer by using a parcel of sphagnum moss wrapped around the stem (the roots emerge from the stem into the moss), or by using a plastic pot, as below.

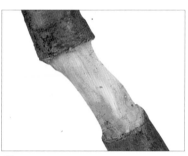

1 △ Use a very sharp knife to make two encircling cuts in the bark, spaced about one and a half times the stem diameter, and remove the bark.

2 △ Cut down one corner of a plastic pot and halfway across the bottom of it towards the centre. Trim to fit around the trunk and fix in place.

3 △ Twist pieces of wire around the pot to hold it firmly in position. Fill it with free-draining soil mixture (the same as that used for cuttings).

Pot rests on the lower branches

THE COMPLETED AIR LAYER △
After the roots have developed, you can sever the stem at the base of the plastic pot and so avoid repotting the new tree.

79 HOW TO GRAFT

This method is particularly appropriate for fruit trees as they take many years of growing before they produce mature flowers and fruit. The section of the tree to be grafted onto the rootstock is called the scion. To make sure the graft will "take", align the cambium layers (green layers under the bark) of the scion and the rootstock.

The green layers are exposed

1 △ First, you need to prepare the scion. Use a very sharp grafting knife, scalpel, or single-edged razor blade to cut a wedge shape into its base.

2 △ Make a clean cut across the stock, then split down the stem with a sharp blade. Insert the scion into the split stem and align the green layers.

3 △ Wind clear plastic tape around the graft to hold it firmly in place. Wrap it round the uncut part of the tree stock and the scion's upper stem.

4 △ The plastic tape stretches with the tree's growth, but remove it after one year. Two years after the grafting the wound has completely healed.

SOME SUITABLE SPECIES

80 FUKIEN TEA

(*Carmona microphylla*, also known as *Ehretia buxifolia*) This evergreen shrub is only suitable for indoor cultivation in temperate climates. Position in full light, but always keep the soil moist. Repot every second year in early spring and feed every two weeks from early spring to autumn, less often in winter.

Small, box-like leaves adapt to bonsai easily

PRUNING

As soon as 6–8 leaves have formed, trim back the new growth to 2–3 leaves. Trim often to keep the foliage compact. Wire woody branches at any time.

81 JAPANESE RED MAPLE

(*Acer palmatum* 'Deshojo') This has brilliant scarlet-coloured foliage in spring. Position in full light, but shield from the hot sun, which causes leaf scorch. Water daily throughout the growing season; sparingly in winter, and feed weekly for a month after the leaf buds open (then fortnightly until late summer). Repot plants every two years.

PRUNING
Trim new growth to 1–2 leaf pairs in spring. In the growing season remove large leaves. Total leaf cutting (see p.52) in midsummer encourages small leaves.

82 BAMBOO

(*Arundinaria nitida*) The multiple trunk style is the best for bonsai. You will need to position this in partial shade, protect from frost, and water at least daily. Every two weeks in spring and summer, give it a high nitrogen feed, and repot every second year in late spring. To propagate, divide rhizomes.

PRUNING
Cut dwarf forms back to ground level every second year in early spring. Control large forms by systematic peeling of the leaf sheaths.

Cut canes back every two years

83 HONEYSUCKLE

(*Lonicera*) This can live in full sun (partial shade in summer), but protect from frost. Water daily throughout the growing season, but sparingly in winter (do not let the soil dry out). Feed every two weeks in summer, and repot every two years in a basic soil mix.

Dwarf Honeysuckle

PRUNING
Treat Dwarf Honeysuckle in the same way as topiary. Constant clipping of the leaves is vital to encourage dense growth. Use scissors to refine the design.

84 SILVER BIRCH

(*Betula pendula*) Position in full sun or partial shade and water daily throughout the growing season; keep moist in winter. Feed every two weeks from one month after the leaves open until late summer. Repot every second year until ten years old.

The trunk gently twists and curves

PRUNING
Prune new shoots back to 2–3 leaves in spring and at other growing periods. Remove large leaves throughout the growing season. Use a wound sealant.

85 TRIDENT MAPLE

(*Acer buergerianum*) This species likes full sun and needs water daily in the growing season. Feed weekly for the first month after leaves appear, then every two weeks until late summer. Repot annually in early spring before the buds open, using a free-draining soil mix.

Long, sturdy roots reach for the soil

PRUNING
Trim new shoots back to 1–2 sets of leaves throughout the growing season. In midsummer carry out leaf cutting (see p.52) on vigorous trees.

86 SATSUKI AZALEA

(*Rhododendron indicum* 'Kaho') This popular bonsai plant should be placed in partial shade and watered at least daily in the growing season, using lime-free water. Keep soil moist at all times. Feed every two weeks from early spring until it flowers. Repot once the flowers have withered.

Flowers hide evergreen, oval leaves

PRUNING
Prune all new shoots after flowering, and secondary shoots more lightly until midsummer. Remove dead flowers after they have faded.

87 COTONEASTER

(*Cotoneaster*) The small leaves and flowers of this shrub make it ideal for a wide range of bonsai styles. Place in full sun, protect from frost, and water daily through the growing season. Keep moist at all times, even in winter. Feed every two weeks until flowering and then once a month until late summer. Repot annually in early spring using a basic soil mix.

10-year old cotoneaster 'Decorus'

PRUNING

Cut back old branches until early spring. Constant scissor trimming (see p.51) of new shoots throughout the growing season encourages dense, twiggy growth.

Clusters of small, green needles

88 ATLAS CEDAR

(*Cedrus atlantica*) This is one of four species of cedar. Like many evergreen conifers, all are suited to bonsai cultivation. Position in full sun all year round, water daily, and feed every two weeks throughout the growing season. Repot every three to five years in spring, using a free-draining soil mix. Sow seeds or take softwood cuttings in spring — hardwood cuttings in autumn. Do any grafting in late summer.

PRUNING

Pinch back new shoots in spring and at any further periods of growth. Do not cut the needles as this will cause the new tips to turn brown and look unsightly.

Leaves have silver undersides

89 ELAEAGNUS

(*Elaeagnus multiflora*) This deciduous shrub bears small, scented cream flowers and tiny, blood-red fruit. It is happy in sun or shade, but you need to water daily throughout the growing season, and feed every two weeks in the summer. Repot every second year in early spring and propagate from softwood cuttings in summer.

PRUNING
You will need to carry out major structural pruning in winter. In the summer constantly shorten new shoots as they develop.

90 BANYAN FIG

(*Ficus retusa*) The small-leaved forms of the fig family are best as bonsai, and you can grow them in most sizes and styles. Figs need warm conditions — minimum temperature of 15°C (60°F). Water generously in summer, and keep moist otherwise. Feed every two weeks in the growing season and repot every second year in spring.

PRUNING
Trim new shoots back to 2–3 leaves throughout the growing season, except where you need extension growth. Use wound sealant.

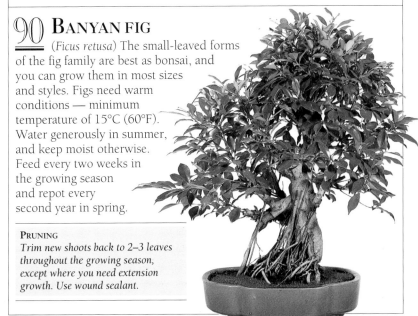

91 WINTER JASMINE
(*Jasminum nudiflorum*)
A deciduous shrub with dark green leaves in spring and summer, especially suited to bonsai. It needs a sunny position shaded from full sun. Water daily in summer and otherwise always keep moist. Feed twice a month, from the end of the flowering until late summer. Repot annually, preferably in autumn.

Flowers grow on previous year's wood

PRUNING
Trim new shoots back to one set of leaves in late spring, and then prune the branches again to 3–4 sets of leaves in the autumn.

Leaves give the tree a delicate appearance

92 HONEY LOCUST
(*Gleditsia triacanthos*) This tree thrives in full sun, but needs frost protection in winter. In the growing season, water daily (sparingly in winter to keep the soil evenly moist), and feed every two weeks. Repot every second year in the spring, using a basic soil mix. Propagate from seeds sown in spring, or from softwood cuttings taken in summer.

PRUNING
In winter, prune branches back hard, or totally remove back to the trunk. New shoots will appear in spring. In summer shorten new shoots as they grow.

93 SCOTS PINE

(*Pinus sylvestris*) Protect from frost and cold winds. Water only when the soil is drying out. Feed every three to four weeks.

Compact needle clusters

Branches wired for downward growth

Scots Pine is ideal for literati style

PRUNING

Pinch off overgrown shoots as needles begin to appear. Remove long primary shoots throughout the growing season. Prune branch tips every second year.

94 CRAB APPLE

(*Malus*) Position in full light all through the year. Water daily in the growing season, especially when the plant is fruiting, or the apples will shrivel and drop.

Fruit appears after flowers

A 'Nagasaki' crab apple tree

PRUNING

It is best to prune this tree in the spring by finger pruning (see p.52) new shoots to 1–2 leaves. Trim back all the long shoots in the autumn.

Heavy pot balances the leaning plant

Japanese Flowering Cherry

PRUNING
Trim plant back after flowering. In summer prune back tips of new shoots as they grow. In winter prune the branches where needed.

95 FLOWERING CHERRY

(*Prunus serrulata*) Place this in full sun, protecting from frost in winter. Water daily throughout the growing season, but sparingly in winter (always keep soil moist). Avoid dropping water onto open flowers as this spoils the petals. Repot annually in late spring or late autumn.

96 WISTERIA

(*Wisteria*) This likes plenty of sun, but protect it from frost in the winter. Water daily throughout the growing season, and always keep the soil moist, even in winter. After flowering has ceased, feed once a week until midsummer. Repeat in the autumn. Repot after flowering every third year, using a basic soil mix. Propagate from hardwood cuttings in late winter or early spring, or by grafting in early spring. Growing from seed takes years.

12-year old Japanese Wisteria

PRUNING
You need to prune wisteria several times a year, beginning in spring, immediately after flowering. Reduce new shoots to 2–3 sets of leaves.

97 ROWAN OR MOUNTAIN ASH

(*Sorbus aucuparia*) A hardy tree which likes full sun. Water daily throughout the growing season, but less frequently in winter (do not let the soil dry out). Feed every two weeks in the growing season. Repot every 1–2 years in spring.

Informal upright style

PRUNING
In order to develop the overall shape, constantly cut back any new growth to one or two leaves (except where you require extension growth).

98 CRAPE MYRTLE

(*Lagerstroemia indica*) In temperate climates, you can grow this outdoors in summer. In winter, keep cool, but frost-free, to allow leaf drop and dormancy. Water daily from spring through autumn, but sparingly during winter dormancy (do not let the soil dry out). Repot annually in early spring in a basic soil mix, and feed every two weeks throughout the growing season. Propagate from seed or softwood cuttings.

PRUNING
Let new shoots extend until late spring, then cut back to 2–3 leaves on each shoot. Flowers appear on new shoots developed after spring pruning.

DISPLAY & ARRANGEMENT

99 INDOOR DISPLAY

Display your bonsai at eye-level against a plain, pale background that does not detract from the tree's natural beauty. Do not stand the pot in a dish for drainage, but water in the garden and drain well before bringing in. Avoid placing the pot near an open fire, by a radiator, on a television set, or on a windowsill (in full sun).

△ TRADITIONAL DISPLAY
This is a Tokonama-style display, where the tree is featured in its own space.

The trunk lines lead the eye from left to right

Pruned trees form silhouettes

◁ LANDSCAPE DISPLAY
This bonsai arrangement (on a large piece of Ibigawa rock) is displayed on a Japanese water tray (suiban).

100 OUTDOOR DISPLAY

Most bonsai are hardy trees which should live permanently outdoors. Position in good light as follows:

- Arranged on shelves attached to a garden wall or the side of a garage.
- Along wooden benches (at table-top height for easy access).
- On a "monkey pole" (vertical pole with a platform on top).
- Along a low garden wall.

△ WATER BASIN
This provides the humid conditions necessary for the rock plantings.

▽ MONKEY POLES
The varying heights of the monkey poles provide a display at different levels.

101 EXHIBITING BONSAI

There are three basic requirements for a full-scale exhibition:

- There should be enough space surrounding each tree.
- It must be possible to see the front view of all the trees.
- The background should be a light, plain colour, high enough to accommodate the tallest bonsai.

△ EXHIBITION ARRANGEMENT
The stand above accommodates both the height and spread of the trees.

INDEX

Acknowledgments

Dorling Kindersley would like to thank Hilary Bird for compiling the index, Ann Kay for proof-reading, and Mark Bracey for computer assistance.

Photography
All photographs by Paul Goff except for: Bill Jordan 53; author 68t and 69c.

Illustrations
David Ashby 38,39